This Coloring Book Belongs To:

I AM
WORTHY
OF LOVE
AND
RESPECT

I AM
STRONG
AND
CAPABLE

I AM
BEAUTIFUL
INSIDE
AND OUT

I HAVE THE
POWER TO
CREATE
POSITIVE
CHANGE IN
MY LIFE

I DESERVE
HAPPINESS
AND
SUCCESS

I EMBRACE MY UNIQUENESS AND INDIVIDUALITY

I TRUST
IN
MYSELF
AND MY
ABILITIES

I
AM A
SURVIVOR

I AM
ENOUGH
JUST AS
I AM

I RADIATE
CONFIDENCE
AND GRACE

I LET GO
OF FEAR
AND
EMBRACE
COURAGE

I AM
A WORK IN
PROGRESS
AND
THAT'S
OKAY

I AM
SUPPORTED
BY THE
UNIVERSE

I
CHOOSE
TO FOCUS
ON THE
GOOD IN
LIFE

I AM A WARRIOR, NOT A VICTIM

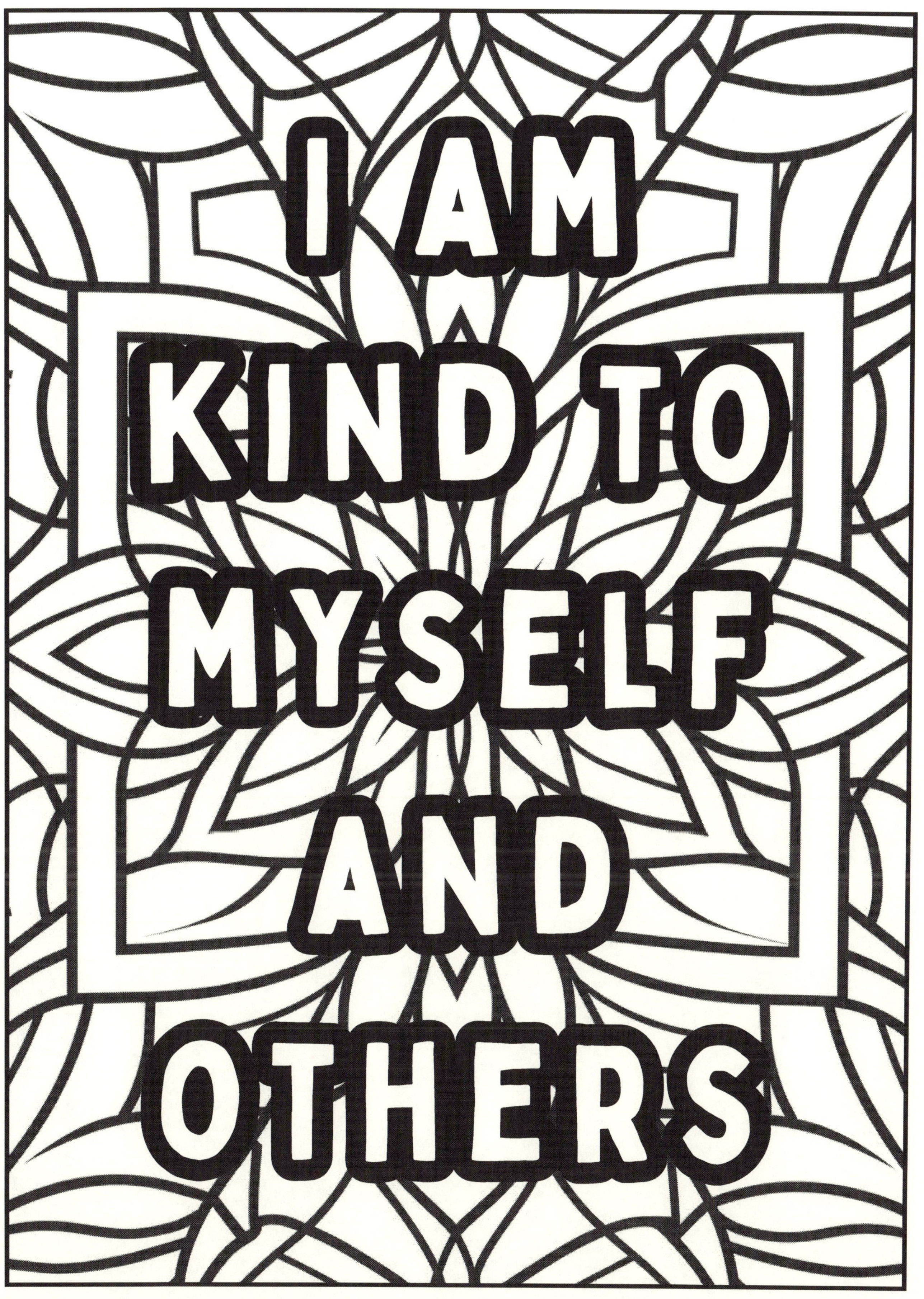

I AM
KIND TO
MYSELF
AND
OTHERS

I AM
GRATEFUL
FOR ALL
THAT I
HAVE

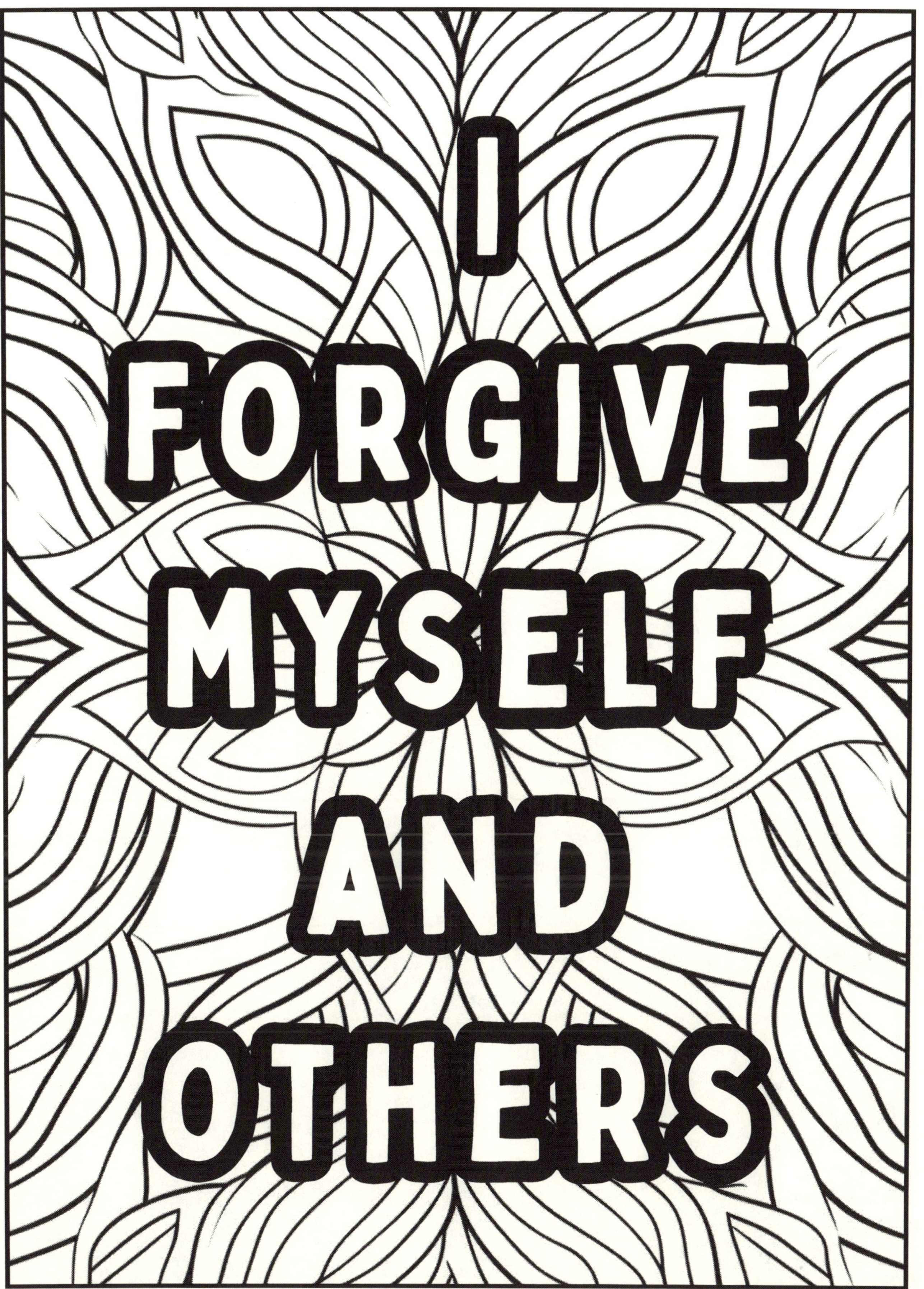

I
FORGIVE
MYSELF
AND
OTHERS

I AM
RESILIENT
AND
ADAPTABLE

I AM
CONSTANTLY
GROWING
AND
EVOLVING

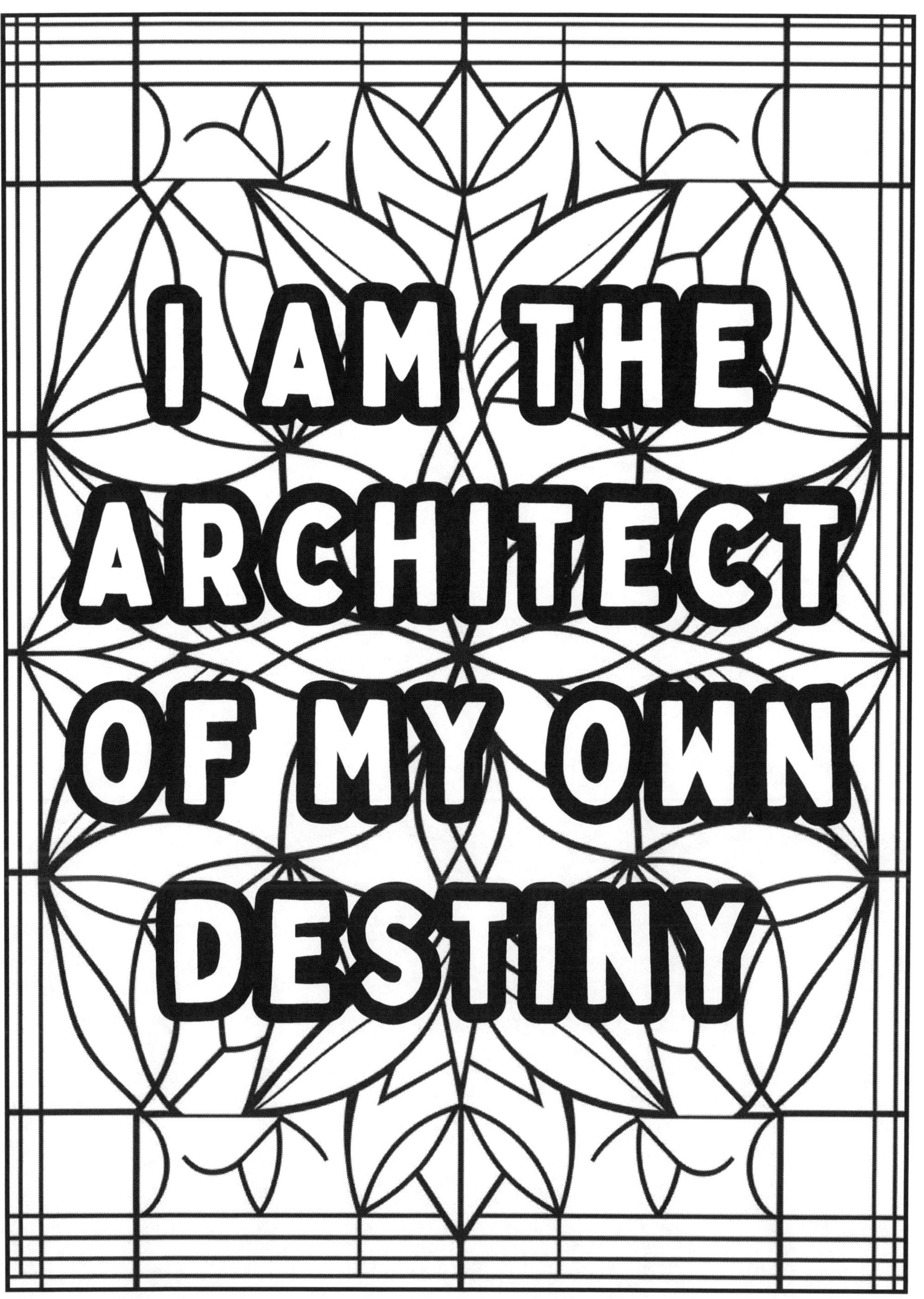

I AM THE
ARCHITECT
OF MY OWN
DESTINY

I RELEASE
NEGATIVITY
AND
WELCOME
POSITIVITY

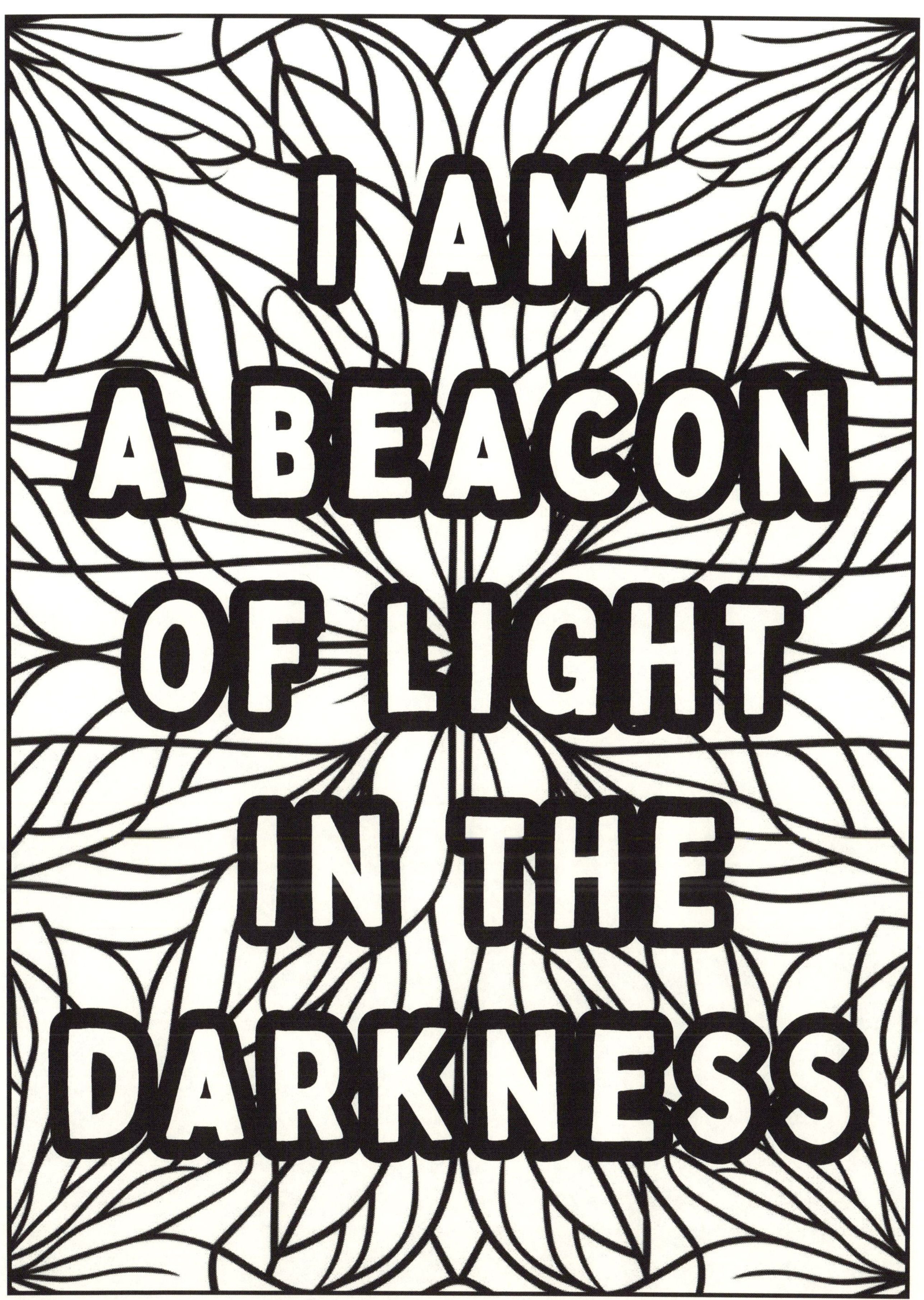
I AM
A BEACON
OF LIGHT
IN THE
DARKNESS

I HONOR
MY
STRENGTH
AND INNER
POWER

I EMBRACE
CHANGE AND
TRANSFORMATION

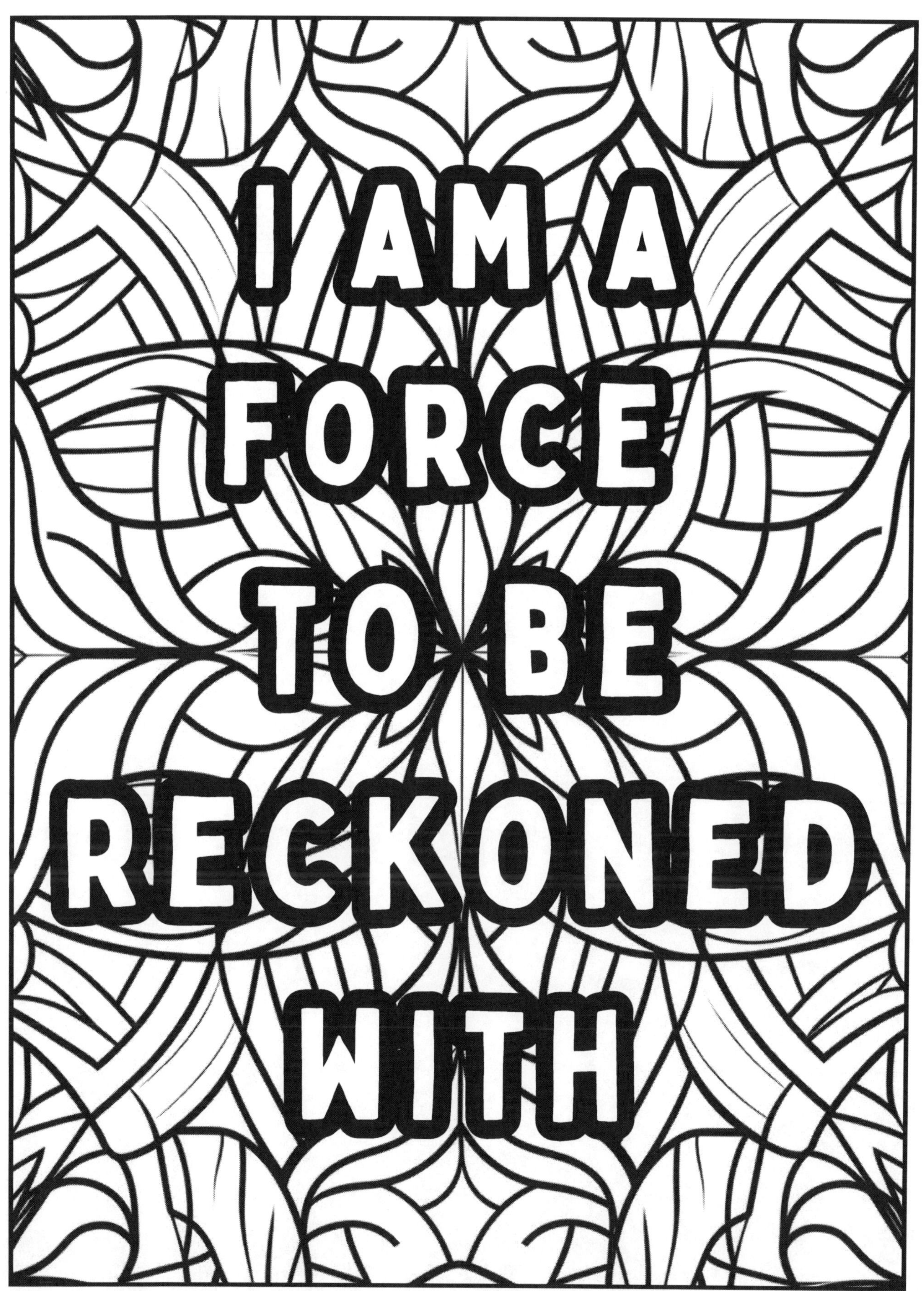

I AM A
FORCE
TO BE
RECKONED
WITH

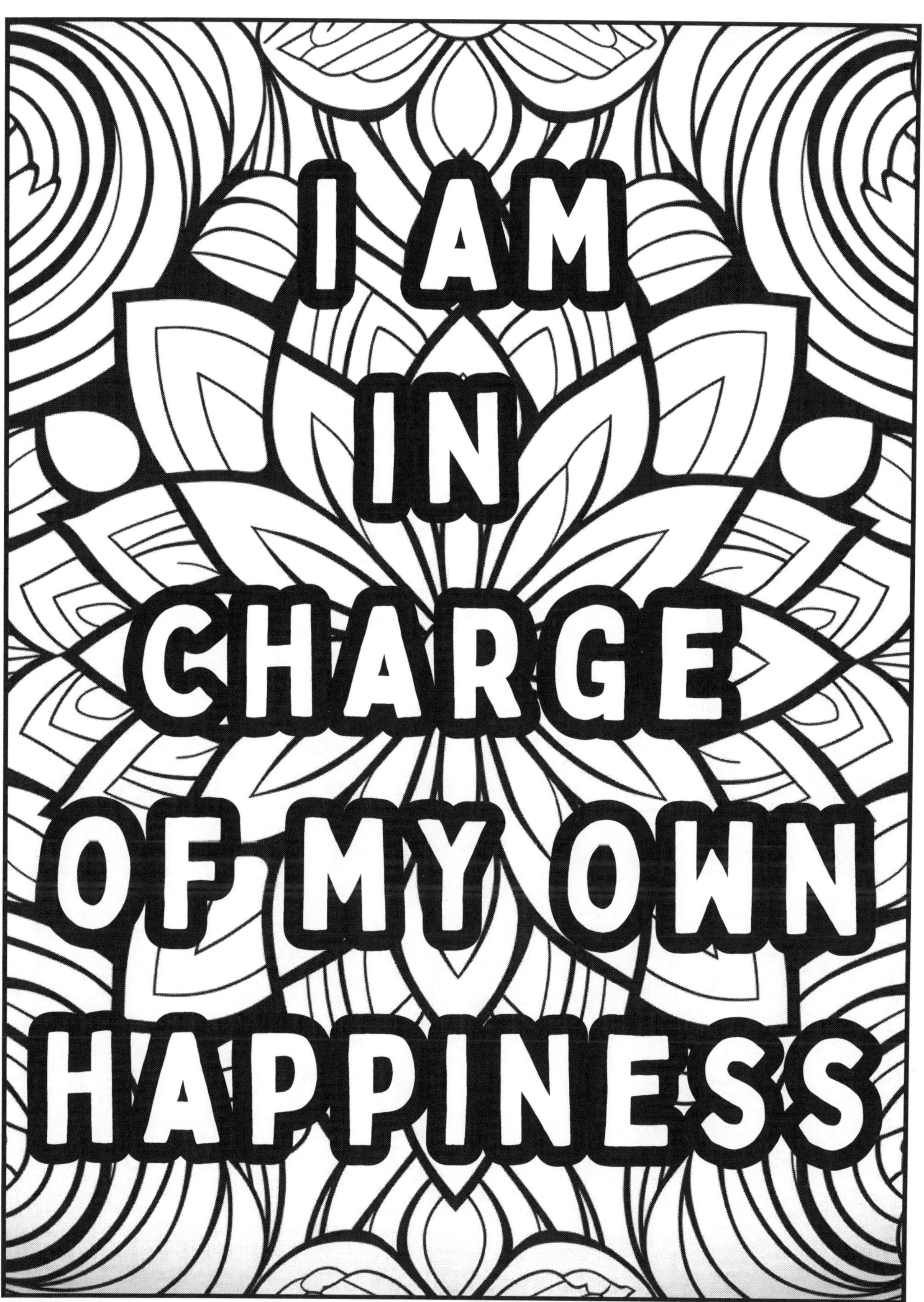
I AM
IN
CHARGE
OF MY OWN
HAPPINESS

I AM
DESERVING
OF
ABUNDANCE
AND
PROSPERITY

I AM
OPEN
TO NEW
POSSIBILITIES
AND
OPPORTUNITIES

I AM A
MASTERPIECE
IN THE
MAKING

Made in the USA
Middletown, DE
28 February 2025